GW00992065

Secrets

Sue Torr MBE

Gate
HOUSE

Secrets
Text copyright © Sue Torr MBE 2006
Edited by Catherine White

Cover design by Ian Bobb
Photograph of the author by Catherine White
Other photographs from Sue Torr's collection
Illustrations by Year 6 Pupils at Mount Wise Primary School, Plymouth
and by Jasmine, Sue Torr's granddaughter

First published and distributed in 2007 by Gatehouse Media Limited

Printed by Taylor Printing Limited, Oldham

ISBN: 978-1-84231-024-3

British Library Cataloguing-in-Publication Data:
A catalogue record for this book is available from the British Library

We have planned the book
so that the left-hand pages
tell my full story.

The right-hand pages
tell my story too,
but in a shorter way.

Shout It Out
If you can't read you can't do it!

I used to think that people who can read are gifted.
They can do anything, be anything,
go anywhere in the world.

If you can't read, you can't do it.
If you can't write and spell, you can't do it.
You can't write a shopping list.
You can't send letters to school.
You can't help your children with their homework.
You can't fill out forms,
find your way around,
write cheques,
write for help
or read recipes.
You can't write letters to your family or friends.
You don't buy books, newspapers or magazines.

It's like you are blind.
You've got no self-esteem.
You can't be yourself.
You're always putting yourself down.
You're always walking away from opportunities.
And so it goes on and on and on.

If you can't read,

there are so many things in life

that you can't do.

It's like you are blind.

You've got no self-esteem.

You always put yourself down.

Yes, I went to school.
Everybody goes to school.
I was there.
So were the others.
They learnt.
I didn't.
I was good at sport.
Everybody knew that.
But nobody knew that I couldn't read or write.
That was my secret.

Every day of my life was frustration,
fear, anger, isolation,
embarrassment and rage.
Dunce, dumbo and bird-brain
were just some of the names I was called.

The day my children started school,
I knew my life would be a nightmare.
I couldn't help them.

Then my life changed.

S. Jorombe.

I could not read.

I could not write or spell very well.

It made life hard for me.

Nobody knew.

That was my secret.

Then my life changed.

Growing Up

I went to school every day, just like everyone else.
I never liked school much. It was always the same
people putting their hands up to answer questions.
The teacher only asked the bright kids to do things.
If you were slow or shy, you were ignored. It was too
much trouble for them to waste time on someone like
me. I was always the one looking around, gazing out
of the windows and watching the clock. I never
thought of school as being important. You just had to
be there.

I know one thing I was good at and that was sport.
I loved square ball, netball, rounders - just anything
to do with sport outside the classroom. I was so
keen on sport that sometimes I would play without
plimsolls, just in bare feet. I put all my energy into it.
It was great.

My parents had eight children - five boys and three
girls - and my mother had to work to support us. She
was a home-help and my father was a painter and
decorator. When they got home from work, there
wasn't time for either of them to sit and read to us.
We never talked about school work.

I went to school

just like everyone else.

I didn't like it.

I gazed around the classroom,

day-dreaming.

But I loved sport so much,

I would play in bare feet.

My school reports were always very poor. They came in a brown envelope, addressed to my parents. But I used to open them. I would show my reports to a friend and she would say, "You're bottom, again." I was always scared to show them to my parents. Sometimes, I lied and said I had lost them.

Charlie and Chris

I had five brothers and two sisters.

My parents were too busy

to help us all with our school work.

My school reports were so bad,

I was scared to show them

to my parents.

I lied and said I had lost them.

Leaving School

I was fifteen when I left school. I remember the last day, walking out through the school gates, feeling all grown up but at the same time feeling empty. I was singing to myself on the way home,
"No more lessons, no more learning.
Won't be long before I'm earning."

When I got home, I went upstairs to my bedroom and lay on my bed, thinking about what kind of job I was going to get. I felt so happy but scared at the same time. All I kept thinking was, "I want to give my mum some money, I want to buy myself some new shoes and I want to go out with my friends just a couple of nights a week. It's not a lot to ask, is it?" But there was nothing I could do, because I couldn't read and write.

I wanted to work in a shop selling clothes and make-up, looking dressed up and gorgeous. When I went to apply for the kind of jobs I really wanted, they'd hand me an application form. I'd take it and feel good taking it, but when I got outside the door I'd rip it up. I'd say to myself, "I'm kidding myself, yet again."

I left school at fifteen.

No more lessons,

no more learning.

Won't be long

before I'm earning.

But I didn't get the jobs

I really wanted.

Jemma

Instead, I went for dead-end jobs - poorly paid jobs, cleaning toilets and washing floors. A friend told me about a job at a flour mill - an extra job, more money - but it was awful. I got flour everywhere on me. When I left to go home, I would hope that I wouldn't see anyone I knew, because they'd know where I worked and I was ashamed and embarrassed.

My worst time was when I was out dancing with my friends, meeting people of my own age. They would ask, "Where do you work?" and I would say I worked as a receptionist or a shop assistant. Lying again!

Then I got a job as a waitress, but every day was a nightmare. I would ask the chef, "What's the special today?"
"Have a look for yourself, it's written on the menu."
But I couldn't read the menu. Sometimes, I would call out my order to the chef and he would shout, "Write it down. Write it down, why don't you!"

So I worked out a sign for each dish. Then, when a customer ordered, I would have to remember the sign. Often, I would memorise the first letter of each dish. I made a lot of mistakes. People would get soup instead of steak.

I got dead-end jobs,

earning poor money.

I cleaned toilets

and washed floors.

I worked in a flour mill.

I was ashamed and embarrassed.

I used to lie to people

about what I did for a living.

As much as I hated my job, I loved meeting people. I was good at that. And I was always happy at the end of the day to go home and think, "I just got through another day without reading a word." This went on for years and years.

I got a job as a waitress.

I couldn't read the menu.

I couldn't write down

what people wanted to eat.

So I made lots of mistakes.

Getting Married

One night, when I went out with my friends, I met
a handsome young man, called David. We got talking
and we started seeing a lot of each other. Always in
the back of my mind, I had my secret. It was like a
shadow hanging over me. At the age of seventeen
I married him. It was a way of getting out of the
work-place (having babies!).

On my wedding day, I was nervous just like any bride
would be, but I was more so because of my secret.
I was more worried about finding out how to write my
middle name on the register than I was about the
most exciting day of my life. I could copy words and
I could write a few I knew, but I'd never had to write
Carole, my middle name.

I asked somebody, "How do you spell *Carole*?"
"What do you want to spell that for?" he asked.
"Because it's my middle name," I answered.
"What, can't you even spell your middle name?"
My face went red and I got that sick feeling in my
stomach again.
"Is it with an 'e' or without?"
Even that threw me. "With an 'e'," I replied. He spelt
it out and I went to my bedroom and quickly wrote

At seventeen, I met David.

Getting married was a way out.

On our wedding day,

I was nervous.

I didn't know how to write *Carole*,

my middle name.

When someone told me,

I wrote it on my hand

so I could copy it onto the register.

Leanne

it out on the palm of my hand. What a relief! When it came to signing the register, I just had to look at my hand to copy it down.

David was in the Royal Navy. I remember the first time he told me he was going to sea. I remember sitting in the doctor's surgery, looking at our wedding photographs, waiting to see the doctor. The doctor called me into his room and told me I was three months pregnant. Wow! I was so happy. But then I thought of my husband going away for a year and me, having the baby on my own. My mind flashed forward to my child starting school, wanting help with his homework and me saying, "Go and ask your dad, I haven't got time."
"These are the words this child will hear," I thought.
I was already planning my excuses, even before the child was born.

Soon after, David went to sea. He sent me letters with kisses and codes on the back - SWALK (Sealed With A Loving Kiss) and BURMA (Be Undressed and Ready My Angel). I looked for ages at the words because I knew what they meant to us. He numbered each letter, which I put in a box. I loved his letters, but I couldn't read them.

David was in the Royal Navy.

I was three months pregnant

when he went to sea,

for a year.

I would have the baby on my own.

The thought scared me.

The future scared me.

When I opened his letters, I would look at the lines of handwriting and pick out words that I knew, to try to make sense of the letter. It was frustrating for me because I would have to think of a way for someone to read them to me, without them thinking I could not read. The fear started again - anxious feelings again.

I would invite a friend in and say, "I've got a letter from David. Have a look whilst I put the kettle on." Or I'd say, "I can't read his handwriting, can you?" "I can't read your husband's letters," she'd say, "because there might be something private in there." "No, it's alright, there won't be anything private." And so she would read it. (Sad really, isn't it?)

I'd listen hard as my friend read his letter out loud. "What shall I write back to him?" "Tell him what you've been up to." "I tell you what, you take the paper and pen. You write faster than me." And she would. That's how I'd get a friend to write some of my letters. I would copy them out later in my own writing.

But when I was on my own, I'd get all of David's letters out of the box, spread them out on the floor and try to put a letter together by copying words that looked familiar to me, from his letters.

David sent me lovely letters,
but I couldn't read them.
I'd make excuses to a friend
so she'd read them out to me.
Then I'd make more excuses
so she'd help me
to write a letter back.
Our first child, Tanya, was born
when he was at sea.
I had so many exciting things
to write to him about.
But I couldn't do it.

I gave birth to our first child, Tanya, when he was at sea. I wanted to tell him about all the fantastic things that were happening at home, but I could only write that something was 'nice'. He complained that I wrote boring letters, but still I didn't tell him. By the time my son came along, six years later, I still hadn't faced up to my problem (you know - my secret).

Sometimes, just to let David think I could read, I would get out a cookery book and say to him, "Have a look and see what you'd like for tea." He would point to something and say, "That looks good. We'll have that." I would copy the recipe out just to let him see me writing. I wanted him to stay around me while I was writing and to feel his eyes on me. We never did have anything from the cookery book. Once I had copied out the recipe, I couldn't read what I had written... so it would be egg, chips and beans or fish fingers, chips and peas, as usual. Luckily his mother lived up the road. She cooked a lot for him.

I like writing. It feels good. I love putting pen to paper. I never knew what I was writing about, I just wanted to write. When I saw people writing, I felt jealous, stupid and left out. I kept wondering what was wrong with me.

I pretended to David

that I could read and write.

I would ask him

to choose something nice for tea

from a cookery book.

I copied out the recipe

but later,

I couldn't read what I had written.

So we had the same things for tea

again and again.

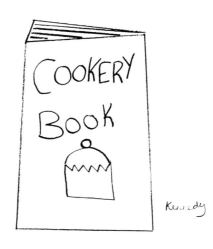

One day, I was sitting on my own with a pen in my hand, trying to write words down in a sentence, when I heard someone coming into my house. I quickly screwed up the paper I was writing on. A friend came in, picked up the screwed up ball of paper and said, "Did you write that? What does it say anyway, I can't understand it?"

"I don't know, it's not mine," I lied. It was mine! I got that anxious feeling again.

I lived with my mother-in-law for a while. One day, I went to sit down but there was a newspaper in the way. As I picked it up, she said, "Sue, what's on the TV tonight?" Fear struck me right away.

"Oh, nothing much."

"What's on BBC2?"

"Just a load of rubbish."

"Oh, there must be something on TV worth watching."

"I'm just going to the toilet."

I was so upset, angry and red-faced, hating my mother-in-law for that moment, for making me feel that worthless feeling again.

David never knew I couldn't read. I was too ashamed to talk about it. I couldn't talk about much really because I never read anything. I just watched TV, listened to the radio and talked with my friends.

I like writing.

I like feeling the pen on the paper.

When I had to read,

a fear would strike me.

Once, I ran upstairs

and locked myself in the toilet,

angry and crying,

feeling worthless.

David read a lot. I used to look at his face when he was reading a book and see his expressions change. I wished I could be part of that world - the reading world. Eventually, we grew apart and, after thirteen years together and two children, we separated.

I moved back home to Plymouth with my children, Tanya and Glen, to live with my mum and dad. I got a job in a pub, just a few yards up the road from mum's house. It was something to do. It got me out. I like being around people. That's when I met up with Brian and had my third child, BJ - but we didn't get married.

I was determined that my children would have a different life. I remembered how, as children, we had hardly any books. I bought lots of books for my children and left them lying around their bedroom, hoping they would be picked up and read.

I knew my eldest son, Glen, could read because he spent a lot of his time in the toilet reading books and newspapers with me outside, hammering on the door. Glen was always reading books. I can remember looking at him sitting on the settee for hours, in another world. I always felt jealous and useless because I wasn't helping him with his education. I wished it was me sitting there with a book and him

I always lied about it.

I lied to everyone.

David never knew I couldn't read.

After many years together,

we didn't talk much.

I had nothing to say.

In the end, we split up.

looking at me. Sometimes, I used to feel like snatching the book out of his hands and telling him to get out and play with his friends. It was my way of crying out for help. I wanted him to help me to read a book.

When my youngest son, BJ, started school, I really wanted to help him with his homework. This one particular day, I did try to help him - in my own way. I thought I had done really well and was feeling quite good about myself. I remember the next day feeling very anxious for him to come home from school. When he came in, I said, "How did you get on with your homework, love?"
"Don't talk to me about homework," he said, "I got it all wrong!"
"At least I tried," I said.

I was 38 when I got a job as a dinner lady at my son's school, Mount Wise Primary School. I loved my dinner lady job. I used to walk around the playground talking to the children. Some children used to come up and hold my hand and sometimes, I wished I had fifteen hands to hold all of them with. Kids would come up and say,
"Miss, can you do up my shoelaces, please?"
"Miss, can you put my hair in a plait?"
It was constantly *Miss* this or *Miss* that.

I got a job as a dinner lady
in my son's school.
I loved the job.
I loved the children.
There were so many
wanting to hold my hands.
I wished I had fifteen hands.

Jemma

The Secret is Out

The only thing I didn't like much was wet playtimes when the children had to stay in their classroom. The children would sit down on the mat with their books and say, "Miss, can you read this book? Miss, can you read that one?"
I would always say, "Put the books down, I have got my own special story I want to tell you."

The children used to love my stories but, one wet playtime, one little girl kept on at me to read her book. She kept pushing it into my hands, saying to me, "Please read it to me, Miss."
So, eventually, I said to her, "Alright then."

The little girl came and sat beside me looking at the book. I opened it and started telling a story. The girl kept looking at me and at the words in the book.
She said, "Miss, you're not reading the words in the book, are you? You're just making your own story up again."
I looked at her and said, "No, I'm not," but I was lying. I felt awful. I thought to myself, I shouldn't be here with these lovely children.
Then she said, "Miss, you can't read, can you?"
I looked at her and I said, "No, I can't."

I didn't like wet playtimes.

The children had to stay inside.

They asked me to read to them.

I pretended to read from books

but I told them made-up stories.

Then one day,

a little girl found me out!

"I'm only nine and I can read and write. You're old and you can't!" I felt worthless.

The next day when I went into work, it was all around the playground that I couldn't read or write. Kids came up to me saying, "You can't read, can you Miss?" Kids were also going up to my son, BJ, and saying, "Your mum's thick." BJ got into fights about it. Kids looked at me like I had some kind of illness. They just couldn't understand it because they think if you're an adult, you know everything.

Some of the children felt sorry for me. In a way, I was relieved that they knew my secret, because the next wet playtime, the children got their spelling books out and each gave me a word to spell on the blackboard. I got two out of fifteen right. I thought they would give me small words to spell like *and, the, then, when* and *look*, but they gave me words like *Mississippi* and *elephant* to spell. I was so shocked, but happy at the same time for them because they can spell. How lucky they are!

I had to admit

that I could not read.

I could not lie any more.

At first, some of the children

would tease my son.

But most of the children were kind.

They began to teach me!

A New Start

As I left the school one day, I bumped into Sue, an adult education worker. She was standing by the school gate, handing out books for parents to read. She gave me a Gatehouse book called 'Never in a Loving Way' by Josie Byrnes. I went straight home and opened it. I looked at all the pictures and tried to recognise the few words I knew - *that, in* and *the*.

When I next saw Sue, she explained that it was her job to help adults with reading difficulties. She asked me how I had got on with the book. I said very quickly and quietly, "I couldn't read some of the words, but the pictures told me a story." I felt so relieved to tell someone about my secret - it was like bricks being lifted off my shoulders. "Can you help me?" I asked. That was the most difficult moment of my life. I was terrified that Sue would laugh at me or tell me I was stupid and I had to keep reminding myself that it was her job to help people like me.

I started having lessons with Sue once a week, then twice and three times a week. When I wrote my first sentence, we both had tears in our eyes. When I read my first book - the one she handed me outside the school gates - I felt so good I wanted to open the

I met Sue,

an adult education worker.

She gave me a book to read.

I took it home and looked at it.

I had to tell Sue

I couldn't read some of the words,

but the pictures told me a story.

It was a relief to tell someone

about my secret.

Sue was very helpful.

She started to teach me.

When I read that first book,

I felt so good.

I wanted to shout it out

to the world.

windows and shout it out to the world.
"Hey, look! I've just read my first book, all by myself, without any help from anyone. I can read!"

Soon, I was going down to see Sue every day, hoping she would give me some more time. We started meeting at the community flat near where I live and where Sue joined the writers' group. The more she taught me, the more I wanted to learn. I was also learning about myself - that I couldn't sit for long, I couldn't concentrate very well, I had to have short breaks, I got headaches and eyestrain. But, on the good side, I was feeling more confident in myself and I had more self-esteem. My whole outlook on life started to change. I was feeling good about myself, for once.

I was demanding so much of Sue's time. One day, she got so fed up with me she said, "Why don't you go home and write down all the things you can't do if you can't read, for homework. Never mind about the spelling, punctuation or grammar. We can correct it all together later."

When she said that to me, that was it. I just kept on thinking about my life - my struggle. I just had to get it out of my head and put it down on paper. Sometimes,

Sue helped me a lot.

The more she helped me,

the more I wanted to learn.

She told me to write a list

of all the things you can't do

if you can't read.

As I wrote, the tears fell.

It was such a relief to get it all out.

I could be doing the dishes when I would think of something and write it down. Often, when I was writing, the tears would be dropping down on the paper. The memories were stirring emotions inside me I never knew I had. It was such a relief to get it down on paper.

Every time I wrote something, Sue and I would go over it and put the spellings, capital letters and full stops in correctly. Then, Sue would type it all up and give it back to me. I would feel very proud and say to Sue, "Did I really write that?"
It gave me a really good feeling inside. I wanted everyone to see what I had written.

Sue showed my work to a lady from the education department of Plymouth Theatre Royal, who suggested that the writers' group put a play together using some of our writing.

A few weeks later, she brought a script based on our writing. As we were looking at it, some people were saying, "I'd like to be in it. I'll take part. I'll read my poem." I thought I couldn't do it because I had never acted in my life before. I'd never even been into a theatre before. Everyone else was up for it, so I had no choice.

Sue typed up my writing.

It looked so good.

It gave me a good feeling inside.

Someone said we should

put it in a play.

I was scared, but I agreed.

Shout It Out

Sue, my tutor, was in the play and so was the local vicar, who used to come to the community flat to write his sermons. We started rehearsals. It was really difficult for me as I could hardly remember my lines. I had to go over them time after time. Sometimes, walking up to the shops or in the park, I would be going over my lines. People who walked past me must have thought I was talking to myself.

Eventually, we were going to perform the play in the local primary school. I remember feeling very nervous about it. The day finally came and all the children, staff and members of the public were there. I was first on stage at the start of the play. I said my first line, looking straight into the headmaster's eyes, and ran off the stage in fright. Someone had to coax me back onto the stage. "Sue, you can do this. Just think of all the thousands of people out there who can't read. You're doing this performance for them."

We went on to perform the play - called *Shout It Out* - in Schools, Young Offenders Institutions, Prisons, Universities, together with Community Centres and Youth Centres. I was amazed at the response from audiences. A child would say, "I wish you could help

We put on our play.

It was called *Shout It Out*.

We put it on in schools,

in community groups,

in young offenders institutions

and in prisons.

People came forward for help.

Jemma

my mum. She can't read." Or an adult would say, "Twenty years of my life have just flashed before my eyes." One of my performances was at Dartmoor Prison, where the inmates' response was, "We might be prisoners here, but you've been a prisoner all your life, inside yourself."

BBC Radio Devon helped us to broadcast the play on the radio. In June 1994, it won a Sony Award. We had a video made of the play. The Shout It Out Project was born - to make people more aware of the importance of education. I simply used my own experiences as an example of what happens to those who have never had the magical feeling of reading a book.

It was about this time I met my second husband, Harry, a college lecturer. It was an exciting time for me. The Basic Skills Agency agreed to fund my project for three years, so I could take my message into schools and colleges and to adult learners around the country.

I am determined to get the message across to non-readers. I want to tell them that they are not backward, stupid or thick. I know what they are going through. I want to show them that their misery doesn't have to last, that they can go and ask for help.

We put the play on BBC Radio.

It won a Sony Award.

We made a video too.

The Shout It Out Project was born.

We were helping people

to face up to their problem

and get help with their reading.

Life is too short

to waste time being ashamed.

But you've got to want to learn.

Meeting the Prime Minister

I first met Tony Blair in the community flat at the end of my newly-designed street, when he was invited to come and look at the refurbishment in progress. Everyone was excited at the prospect of meeting him.

I remember looking at him up and down, thinking how handsome he was, with big blue eyes and a lovely white smile. While we were having a cup of tea together, I was asked if I would take him to look round my flat. I was shocked as I hadn't cleaned or done any preparation and the washing machine was sticking out, waiting to be repaired.

We walked down the street together, surrounded by lots of security men and the press. He went into every room in my flat. I felt very embarrassed each time he opened a door. When we went into my bedroom, we watched out of the window as the press took photos of our great new street. It was an honour to meet him.

I have met Mr. Blair several times since. He once presented me with a book at a 'working breakfast' I went to at Downing Street, with Linda Gilroy MP.

I first met Prime Minister Tony Blair
when he came to see
our new street.
We had a cup of tea together.
He came to look round my flat.
I was embarrassed
because I hadn't cleaned it.
But it was an honour to meet him.

Buckingham Palace

One morning, I was still in bed when the post came. Harry picked the mail up and noticed that there was a crest on one of the letters. "You had better open this one, it looks official," he said. But I asked him to open it for me. He started to read it. "Oh my God, Sue," he cried, "You've had your name put forward to Her Majesty The Queen for an MBE, for Outstanding Service to the Community. You can't tell anyone about it. You must keep it a secret."

Harry was so proud of me he went out and bought me a big bunch of flowers. I felt fantastic. I was giving a speech in London when it was formally announced. Afterwards, I got cards full of congratulations and flowers. The Dingles store in Plymouth offered to rig me out with something to wear for the day. I could go in and pick any outfit, shoes, hat, scarf, gloves - anything I wanted. I walked out with hundreds of pounds' worth of clothing. When I left the shop, I felt so guilty that people might think I'd been shoplifting. As I walked to the bus stop, I remember looking at my reflection in the shop windows, carrying all these bags and a big hat box. When I got home, I laid everything out on my bed and showed all my neighbours.

A letter came in the post.

It was from the Queen.

It said I was to get an MBE.

I was so excited

but I had to keep it secret for now.

The day before the presentation I had a make-over and hairdo. Then, I travelled to London with my three children and we stayed overnight in a hotel near Buckingham Palace.

The next morning, we got into a taxi. The driver said, "Where to, love?"
"To Buckingham Palace!" I replied.
We all looked at each other and burst out laughing. It all seemed so unreal.

Going into the Palace and up the wide, carpeted staircase, I saw a lady in front of me, wearing the same hat as me. I tapped her on the shoulder, she turned round and we both laughed.

His Royal Highness Prince Charles presented me with my MBE on behalf of Her Majesty The Queen. An orchestra played. I had to curtsey and walk away backwards. Afterwards, I had my photograph taken. It was marvellous.

I went to London.

I went to Buckingham Palace.

Prince Charles gave me
my award.

It was a very proud day
for me and my family
I'll remember it forever.

And Now

I got a phone call one day from a lady from Paris. She worked for UNESCO. She invited me to go Paris and give a talk about what it is like to go through life, not being able to read. I have also been on speaking tours to Japan, Sweden, Thailand and West Africa.

I still perform a version of my play - the *Roadshow* - in primary schools. I know that there are thousands of people out there who are struggling with their reading, writing and spelling. I want people to point to me and say, "That's her who couldn't read."

I recently saw a little advertisement in my local newspaper from a girl, thanking me. She had seen my play and was now learning to read and write. I nearly cried when I read it. This is what I am all about.

I shall keep on campaigning to get as many people as possible, of all ages, to come forward for help with their literacy problems. Getting an education is so important because without it, you just exist. You're never too old to learn. I still go to literacy classes. I got my Literacy Level 1 - which I am really proud of - and I am now doing my Level 2. There is still room for improvement.

I have given talks
around the world for UNESCO.
I still perform my play.
I want to help people
who can't read.
I still go to classes.
I still want to get better.

What difference has learning to read and write meant to me?

I've got more confidence in myself.
I don't feel ashamed of myself any more.
My whole outlook on life has changed.
I am a much happier person.
I enjoy what I am doing with my life.

Getting an education was everything for me.
Without it, I just existed.

God, it's good being able to read!

But...

I wish I had paid more attention and put my hand up and asked for help when I was at primary school.

Who would have thought it?

Me, the dunce, the dumbo,

the bird-brain,

writing my very own book!

Ha! Ha!

I've done it!

And I'm smiling.

What a feeling.

What an achievement.

I feel very proud of myself.

Yes, I've done it!

This is the first piece of writing I did, which my tutor, Sue, typed up for me. I drew a picture of my garden.

OUR GARDEN

Dec 92

I can remember living in a house in Swilly, right.
It had a front and back garden.
In the back garden it had a big shed.

Me and my sister and my friends, we used to play shops.
We used stones for money, and I can remember going into the kitchen
and taking everything out of the boxes,
      so I could take them up the shed and sell them.

We had a swing in the back garden where it was used so much,
by all of us children that there was a big crack in the ground.
And I can remember swinging on it and thinking that one day,
the swing's gonna fall down. But it never did.

I can remember, in the front garden there used to be a bar.
I used to swing around the bar, swinging on my stomach.
I can remember my Mum calling, "Get off that bar!"
I didn't hurt myself much, just sort of bruised a bit.

We moved from that house. I suppose I was about twelve.
We couldn't afford to hire a van.
                My Dad borrowed a friend's open van.
My brothers and I sat amongst all the furniture,
going around the round-abouts, catching hold of the furniture
as it was about to fall.

        The new home had no garden.
            I didn't know what to do with myself.

by SUE TORR

Some of my writing for this book:

13 June 06

By the time my son came along six years later,
I still hadn't faced up to my problem of not being
able to read.
    I never even told my husband.
Just to let him think I could read I would get out
a cookery book out, he liked to cook, I would say
to him have a look and see what you would like for
tea, he would look at the book and say that looks
good we well have that I would copy it out on to paper
just to let him see me writing, we never did have
any thing to eat from the cookery Book, Once I copied the
recipe the next day I could not read what
I had written down, so it would be chip egg
and Beans or Fish finger chips and Pea,
One day I was writing to my self I like writing
it feels good I Loved putting pen to paper I never
Know what I was writing about, I just wanted to
Write,... When I see people writing I always feel
Lefe out where did it go wrong for me and the
thousands of other just like me. (Sad)
One day I was writing I heard some one coming in to
my house so I screwed up the paper I was writing was
writing on and a friend come in and pick up the paper
and said did you write that I said no
    he said what's it say any way I cant
under stand it. Well its not mine — trying
again, it was —

    S. Jowno̅se

©

58

Notes from my children, Glen and Tanya.

Sue *can* Read
Sue can write too.
A mother to me
An inspiration to you.

Glen

Thankyou for making me smile everyday,
and making me laugh all the time,
I love you muvver

Tanya.
xxx

Here are a few quotes from the thousands of letters Sue has received after performing the Roadshow in primary schools:

"10 out of 10 - excellent. Amazing. Fantastic."

"I liked every single crumb of the play because it showed me how important it is to put your hand up and tell the teacher."

"You should never laugh at someone who can't spell because they will have bad feelings about spelling."

"I think that it was very interesting and funny."

"I think it was good because it makes me feel that I have to read everyday and whenever I get stuck, I should put my hand up."

"I liked the play because it made me realise that when I am stuck I should not be afraid to put my hand up and ask for help. I should face my problem."

"It shows that you shouldn't be scared to say that you can't read or write."

"It was an important message that if you can't read you can't do lots of things."

"Can you help me?"

"I wish you could come and meet my mum. She can't read."

"It really seemed to strike a chord with many of the children watching to think that an adult could have problems with reading and the impact it can have on your life."
Chris West, Headteacher
Mount Wise Primary School 15.12.06

"The 80 children enjoyed the play at their level and it provoked much conversation and reflection upon the situation that your character experienced in the play. More that 20 adults watched the play... and they cannot fail to have been impressed by the bravery that it eventually took to seek help. I feel that if anybody needed that extra push to force themselves to find help, this play would provide it."
Mr B J Gill, Headteacher
St. Joseph's Catholic Primary School 26.05.06

"We were delighted to be involved in such an exciting and informative 'première'. You gave us much to think about and be aware of - and for this we are grateful."
Winefride Chapple, Chair of Governors
St. Joseph's Catholic Primary School 23.05.06

If you would like to book a performance of the Roadshow or if you wish to support the Shout Project, please telephone 0795 082 6214 or email: suetorr_mbe@yahoo.co.uk

Why can't you spell, Mum?

If you're a parent who can't read, write or spell and you have children who can, you always ask them to help you with words you can't spell. And over the years of asking them, they get more and more uppity with you and they say things like, "What are you, Mum? Dyslexic? Why can't you read and spell? Why have you always got to ask me all the time? Go and ask someone else." But you can't. You don't want anyone else to know.

Non-readers get labelled dunce, dim, backward and brain-dead. You live with the name calling at school, but when your own children call you names like that, it's like a knife going through your heart. And you won't cry in front of them because it hurts so much... and you don't want them to see you crying, so you cry alone.

I've got to stop writing now because I can't see for crying. It's been very hard for me to write things down about me and my family.

Written by Sue Torr on 27th January 1993

Author's Note

I wish to thank the children of Mount Wise Primary School for encouraging me to seek help. I also wish to thank all the people who have inspired me and played an important part in my life. I particularly want to thank:

*Sue Cousins, Ruth Jordan, Tanya, Glen and BJ,
Joanna Haynes, Josie Byrnes, Helen Scott,
Dee Evans, Harry Lapping, Roma French,
Jackie Bonnie, Alan Wells OBE, Keith Scott,
Marie Taylor, Jess Curtis, Ian Phillips,
Linda Gilroy MP, Pembroke Street EMB,
Hamoaze House, The Shekinah Mission,
The Delta Kappa Gamma Society International,
the staff of Plymouth Community Partnership,
the staff of Learning Links,
all my tutors who have helped me to get a better
education and all the volunteers who give up
hundreds of hours of their time to help people with
reading and writing difficulties.*

I hope whoever reads this book can sit back and give a thought to all the people who can't read. Imagine what their life must be like without books.

Gatehouse Books®

Our writers are adults who are developing their basic reading and writing skills. Their ideas and experiences make fascinating material for any reader, but are particularly relevant for adults working on their own reading and writing skills. The writing often strikes a chord with the reader - a shared experience of struggling against many odds.

The format of a Gatehouse Adult Beginner Reader is clear and uncluttered. The language is familiar and the text is often line-broken, so that each line ends at a natural pause.

Gatehouse Books are widely used within Adult Basic Education throughout the English speaking world. They are also a valuable resource within the prison education and probation services, social services and secondary schools.

Available from
Gatehouse Media Limited
PO Box 965
Warrington
WA4 9DE

Tel: 01925 267778
E-mail: info@gatehousebooks.com
Website: www.gatehousebooks.com

and from
avantibooks limited
The iO Centre
Unit 9 Whittle Way
Arlington Business Park
Stevenage
SG1 2BD